JANUARY 2022

February 2022
Su	Mo	Tu	We	Th	Fr	Sa
		1	2	3	4	5
6	7	8	9	10	11	12
13	14	15	16	17	18	19
20	21	22	23	24	25	26
27	28					

Sunday	Monday	Tuesday	Wednesday	Thursday	Friday	Saturday
30/1	31/1					1 NEW YEAR'S DAY
2	3	4	5	6 Holy Three Kings Day (DE) Epiphany (CA)	7	8
9	10	11	12	13	14	15
16	17 Martin Luther King Jr. Day (US)	18	19	20	21	22
23	24	25	26	27	28	29

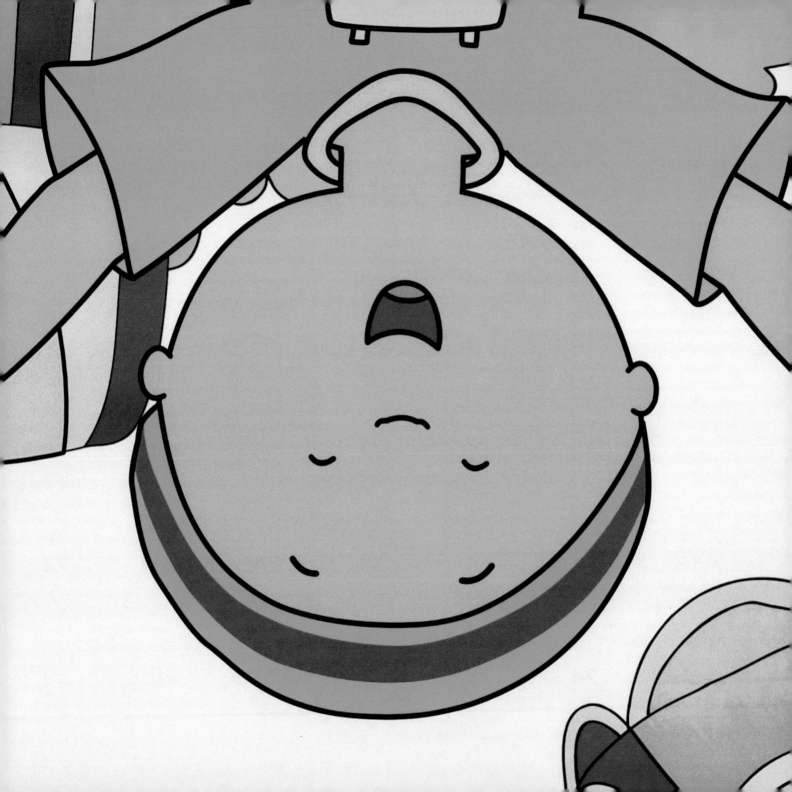

FEBRUARY 2022

March 2022
Su	Mo	Tu	We	Th	Fr	Sa
		1	2	3	4	5
6	7	8	9	10	11	12
13	14	15	16	17	18	19
20	21	22	23	24	25	26
27	28	29	30	31		

Sunday	Monday	Tuesday	Wednesday	Thursday	Friday	Saturday
		1 Chinese New Year	2 Groundhog Day (US/CA)	3	4	5
6	7	8	9	10	11	12 Lincoln's Birthday (US)
13	14 VALENTINE'S DAY	15 National Flag (CA)	16	17	18	19
20	21 Presidents' Day (US)	22	23	24	25	26
27 Carnival (UK)	28 Shrove Monday (DE)					

MARCH 2022

April 2022
Su	Mo	Tu	We	Th	Fr	Sa
					1	2
3	4	5	6	7	8	9
10	11	12	13	14	15	16
17	18	19	20	21	22	23
24	25	26	27	28	29	30

Sunday	Monday	Tuesday	Wednesday	Thursday	Friday	Saturday
		1 Carnival / Shrove Tuesday (DE)	2 Carnival / Ash Wednesday (DE)	3	4	5
6	7	8 International Women's Day	9	10	11	12
13	14 Commonwealth Day (CA)	15	16	17 St. Patrick's Day	18	19
20	21	22	23	24	25	26
27 Mothering Sunday (UK)	28	29	30	31		

APRIL 2022

May 2022

Su	Mo	Tu	We	Th	Fr	Sa
1	2	3	4	5	6	7
8	9	10	11	12	13	14
15	16	17	18	19	20	21
22	23	24	25	26	27	28
29	30	31				

Sunday	Monday	Tuesday	Wednesday	Thursday	Friday	Saturday
					1 April Fool's Day	**2**
3	**4**	**5**	**6** Tartan Day (CA)	**7**	**8**	**9** Vimy Ridge Day (CA)
10 Palm Sunday (DE)	**11**	**12**	**13**	**14** Maundy Thursday (DE)	**15** GOOD FRIDAY	**16** Holy Saturday (DE)
17 EASTER SUNDAY	**18** EASTER MONDAY	**19**	**20**	**21**	**22** Earth Day	**23**
24	**25**	**26**	**27**	**28**	**29**	**30**

MAY
2022

June 2022
Su	Mo	Tu	We	Th	Fr	Sa
			1	2	3	4
5	6	7	8	9	10	11
12	13	14	15	16	17	18
19	20	21	22	23	24	25
26	27	28	29	30		

Sunday	Monday	Tuesday	Wednesday	Thursday	Friday	Saturday
1 Labor Day (DE)	2 May Day (UK)	3	4	5 Cinco De Mayo (US)	6	7
8 End of World War II (DE) Mother's Day	9	10	11	12	13	14
15	16	17	18	19	20	21 Armed Forces Day (US)
22	23 Victoria Day (CA)	24	25	26 Father's Day (DE) Ascension Day (UK/DE)	27	28
29	30 Memorial Day (US)	31				

JUNE 2022

July 2022

Su	Mo	Tu	We	Th	Fr	Sa
31					1	2
3	4	5	6	7	8	9
10	11	12	13	14	15	16
17	18	19	20	21	22	23
24	25	26	27	28	29	30

Sunday	Monday	Tuesday	Wednesday	Thursday	Friday	Saturday
			1	2 Spring Bank Holiday (UK)	3 Platinum Jubilee Bank Holiday (UK)	4
5 Pentecost (US) Whit Sunday (UK/DE)	6 Pentecost Monday (US) Whit Monday (UK/DE)	7	8	9	10	11
12	13	14 Flag Day (US)	15	16	17	18
19 Father's Day	20	21 National Indigenous Peoples Day (CA) June Solstice (CA)	22	23	24	25
26	27	28	29	30		

JULY
2022

August 2022

Su	Mo	Tu	We	Th	Fr	Sa
	1	2	3	4	5	6
7	8	9	10	11	12	13
14	15	16	17	18	19	20
21	22	23	24	25	26	27
28	29	30	31			

Sunday	Monday	Tuesday	Wednesday	Thursday	Friday	Saturday
31/7					1 Canada Day (CA)	2
3	4 Independence Day (US)	5	6	7	8	9
10	11	12	13	14	15	16
17	18	19	20	21	22	23
24 Parents' Day (US)	25	26	27	28	29	30

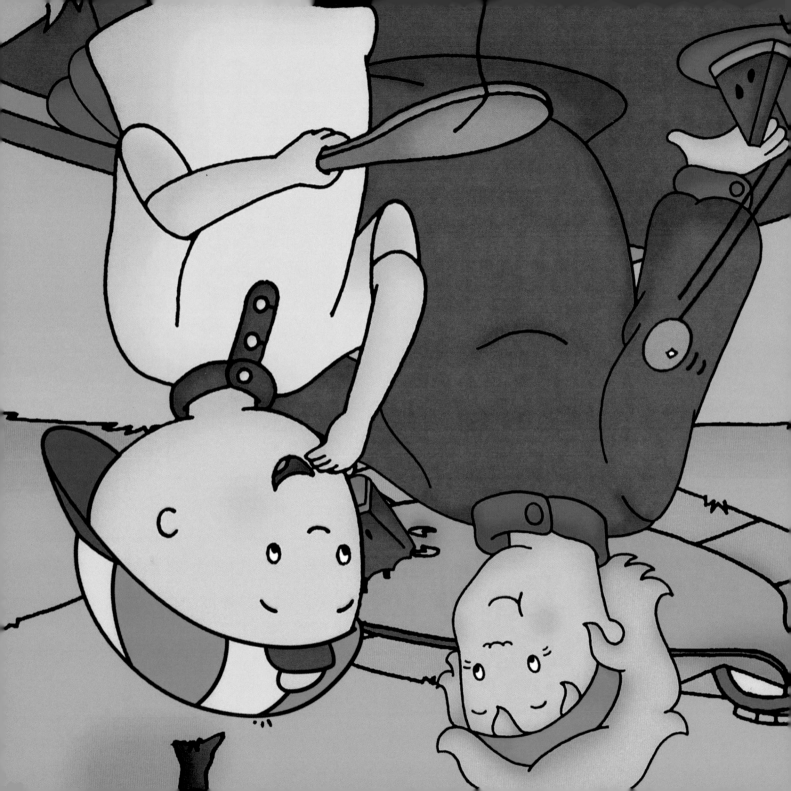

AUGUST 2022

September 2022
Su	Mo	Tu	We	Th	Fr	Sa
				1	2	3
4	5	6	7	8	9	10
11	12	13	14	15	16	17
18	19	20	21	22	23	24
25	26	27	28	29	30	

Sunday	Monday	Tuesday	Wednesday	Thursday	Friday	Saturday
	1	2	3	4	5	6
7	8	9	10	11	12	13
14	15 Assumption of Mary (DE)	16	17	18	19	20
21	22	23	24	25	26	27
28	29 Summer Bank Holiday (UK)	30	31			

SEPTEMBER 2022

October 2022

Su	Mo	Tu	We	Th	Fr	Sa
30	31					1
2	3	4	5	6	7	8
9	10	11	12	13	14	15
16	17	18	19	20	21	22
23	24	25	26	27	28	29

Sunday	Monday	Tuesday	Wednesday	Thursday	Friday	Saturday
				1	2	3
4	5 Labor Day (CA/US)	6	7	8	9	10
11 Patriot Day (US)	12	13	14	15	16	17
18	19	20	21	22 September Equinox (CA)	23	24
25	26	27	28	29	30 National Day for Truth and Reconciliation (CA)	

OCTOBER 2022

Sunday	Monday	Tuesday	Wednesday	Thursday	Friday	Saturday
30/10	31/10 Halloween					1
2 Thanksgiving (DE)	3 Day of German Unity (DE)	4	5	6	7	8
9	10 Thanksgiving Day (CA) Columbus Day (US)	11	12	13	14	15
16	17	18	19	20	21	22
23	24	25	26	27	28	29

NOVEMBER 2022

December 2022

Su	Mo	Tu	We	Th	Fr	Sa
				1	2	3
4	5	6	7	8	9	10
11	12	13	14	15	16	17
18	19	20	21	22	23	24
25	26	27	28	29	30	31

Sunday	Monday	Tuesday	Wednesday	Thursday	Friday	Saturday
		1 All Saints' Day (CA/DE)	2 All Souls' Day (CA)	3	4	5
6	7	8 National Aboriginal Veterans Day (CA)	9	10	11 Veterans' Day (US) St. Martin's Day (DE) Remembrance Day (CA)	12
13 National Day of Mourning (DE)	14	15	16	17	18	19
20 Dead Sunday (DE)	21	22	23	24 Thanksgiving (US)	25 Black Friday	26
27 First Advent Sunday	28 Cyber Monday	29	30 St Andrew's Day (UK)			

DECEMBER 2022

January 2023

Su	Mo	Tu	We	Th	Fr	Sa
1	2	3	4	5	6	7
8	9	10	11	12	13	14
15	16	17	18	19	20	21
22	23	24	25	26	27	28
29	30	31				

Sunday	Monday	Tuesday	Wednesday	Thursday	Friday	Saturday
				1	2	3
4 Second Advent Sunday	5	6 Saint Nicholas Day (DE)	7 Pearl Harbor Remembrance Day (US)	8	9	10
11 Third Advent Sunday Anniversary of the Statute of Westminster (CA)	12	13	14	15	16	17
18 Fourth Advent Sunday	19	20	21 December Solstice (CA)	22	23	24 CHRISTMAS EVE
25 CHRISTMAS DAY	26 Kwanzaa (CA) Boxing Day (CA/UK/DE)	27	28	29	30	31 NEW YEAR'S EVE

2023

JANUARY

Sunday	Monday	Tuesday	Wednesday	Thursday	Friday	Saturday
1 NEW YEAR'S DAY	2 'NEW YEAR'S DAY' DAY OFF	3	4	5	6 Holy Three Kings Day (DE) Epiphany (CA)	7
8	9	10	11	12	13	14
15	16 Martin Luther King Jr. Day (US)	17	18	19	20	21
22	23	24	25	26	27	28
29	30	31				

FEBRUARY

Sunday	Monday	Tuesday	Wednesday	Thursday	Friday	Saturday
			1	2 Groundhog Day (CA/US)	3	4
5	6	7	8	9	10	11
12 Lincoln's Birthday (US)	13	14 Valentine's Day	15	16	17	18
19 Carnival (UK)	20 Shrove Monday (DE) Presidents' Day (US)	21 Carnival / Shrove Tuesday (DE)	22 Carnival / Ash Wednesday (DE)	23	24	25
26	27	28				

MARCH

Sunday	Monday	Tuesday	Wednesday	Thursday	Friday	Saturday
			1	2	3	4
5	6	7	8 International Women's Day	9	10	11
12	13 Commonwealth Day (CA)	14	15	16	17 St. Patrick's Day	18
19 Mothering Sunday (UK)	20	21	22	23	24	25
26	27	28	29	30	31	

APRIL

Sunday	Monday	Tuesday	Wednesday	Thursday	Friday	Saturday
30/4						1 April Fools' Day
2 Palm Sunday (DE)	3	4	5	6 Maundy Thursday (DE) Tartan Day (CA)	7 Good Friday	8 Holy Saturday (DE)
9 Easter Sunday Vimy Ridge Day (CA)	10 Easter Monday	11	12	13	14	15
16	17	18	19	20	21	22 Earth Day
23	24	25	26	27	28	29

Made in the USA
Monee, IL
04 February 2022